Contents

There are many types of animals.

910

This book to be returned on or before the last date below.

Creature

S

www.heinemann.co.uk/library

Visit our website to find out more information about Heinemann Library books.

To order:
☎ Phone 44 (0) 1865 888066
Send a fax to 44 (0) 1865 314091
📄 Visit the Heinemann Bookshop at www.heinemann.co.uk/library to browse our
💻 catalogue and order online.

First published in Great Britain by Heinemann Library,
Halley Court, Jordan Hill, Oxford OX2 8EJ, part of Harcourt
Education. Heinemann is a registered trademark of Harcourt
Education Ltd.

© Harcourt Education Ltd 2007
First published in paperback in 2007
The moral right of the proprietor has been asserted.

Editorial: Tracey Crawford, Cassie Mayer, Dan Nunn,
and Sarah Chappelow
Design: Jo Hinton-Malivoire
Picture Research: Tracy Cummins, Tracey Engel,
and Ruth Blair
Production: Duncan Gilbert

Originated by Chroma Graphics (Overseas) Pte. Ltd
Printed and bound in China by South China
Printing Company

ISBN 978 0 431 18227 8 (hardback)
11 10 09 08 07
10 9 8 7 6 5 4 3 2 1

ISBN 978 0 431 18350 3 (paperback)
12 11 10 09 08
10 9 8 7 6 5 4 3 2 1

British Library Cataloguing in Publication Data

Crawford, Tracey
  Snakes. - (Creature comparisons)
  1.Snakes - Juvenile literature
  I.Title
  597.9'6

Acknowledgements

The publishers would like to thank the following for permission to
reproduce photographs: Corbis pp. 4 (monkey, Frank Lukasseck/
zefa; bird, Arthur Morris), 9 (Michael & Patricia Fogden), 12 (Theo
Allofs), 13, 15 (Michael & Patricia Fogden), 22 (Horned Adder,
Gallo Images; rattlesnake, Jeff Vanuga); Getty Images pp. 4 (fish), 7
(Jim Merli), 10 (The Image Bank/Gallo Images-Anthony Bannister),
23 (king snake, Jim Merli; hatchling, The Image Bank/Gallo
Images-Anthony Bannister); Minden Pictures pp. 11 (Michael &
Patricia Fogden); Carlton Ward pp. 4 (frog), 5, 6, 14, 16, 17, 18,
19, 20, 21, 23 (viper headshot).

Cover photograph of an emerald tree boa reproduced with
permission of Corbis/Joe MacDonald and an Indian cobra
reproduced with permission of Ardea/M. Watson. Back cover
photograph of a banded sea snake reproduced with permission of
Corbis.

Every effort has been made to contact copyright holders of any
material reproduced in this book. Any omissions will be rectified in
subsequent printings if notice is given to the publishers.

Snakes are one type of animal.

Snakes are reptiles.

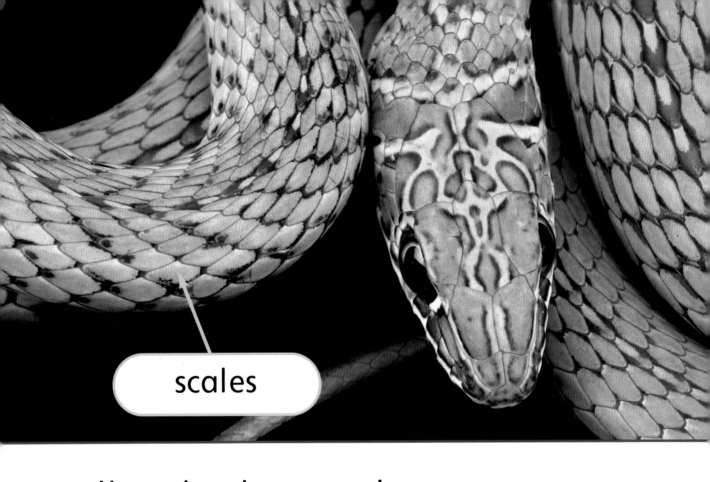

scales

All snakes have scales.

All snakes shed their skin.

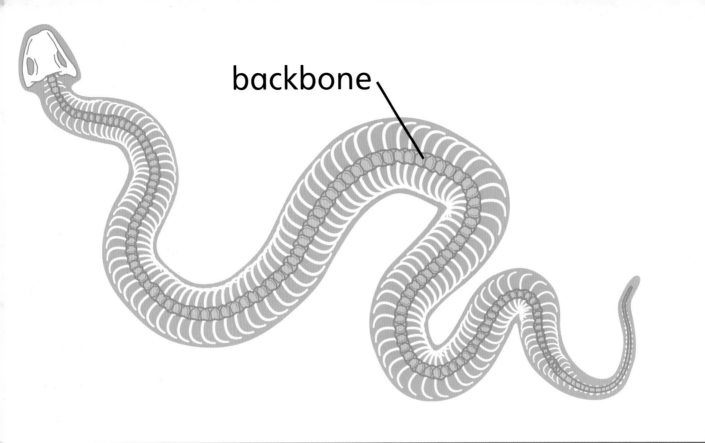

backbone

All snakes have a backbone.

All snakes hunt for food.

Most snakes hatch from an egg.

baby snake

But this snake does not.

Most snakes live on land.

But this snake does not.

Some snakes are big.

Some snakes are small.

Some snakes are smooth.

Some snakes are rough.

Some snakes are one colour.

Some snakes are many colours.

Every snake is different.

Every snake is special.

Snake facts

Snakes cannot hear. Snakes can feel movement.

This snake is a horned viper. It hides itself in the sand.

Picture glossary

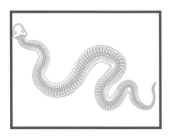

backbone the part of the skeleton that goes from the head to the tail

hatch to be born from an egg

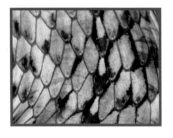

scale a small, flat plate on the outside of an animal. Scales cover skin.

shed to take off

Index

Notes to parents and teachers
Before reading
Talk to the children about snakes. Does anyone keep a pet snake? Has anyone seen a snake in a reptile house?

After reading
Draw a spiral snake: Draw the head at the centre of the spiral and make the end of the spiral the snake's tail. Tell the children to colour a pattern on the snake's skin using diamond patterns. Cut out the spiral and suspend the "snakes" from the ceiling using cotton thread and blue tac.
Say this snake rhyme: "I saw a slippery slithery snake, slide through the grass and down to the lake. He slithered here, He slithered there. That slippery snake slithered everywhere."
Encourage the children to extend the "s" sound at the beginning of the words to sound like snakes.
Explain to the children that snakes move by rippling their bodies. Tell them to stand in a line and to hold hands with their arms extended. Start the ripple by raising your left hand and a child's right hand. As your hands are lowered then that child should lift his left hand and pass the ripple on.

8. Judge and Knapp, p. 149.
9. A. Maynard, 'The Regulation of Public and Private Health Care Markets', in *The Public/Private Mix for Health: The Relevance and Effects of Change*, ed. G. McLachlan and A. Maynard (The Nuffield Provincial Hospitals Trust, London, 1982), p. 484.
10. A. Maynard, 'Privatizing the National Health Service', *Lloyds Bank Review*, no. 148 (1983), pp. 28–40.
11. M. Friedman and R. Friedman, *Free to Choose* (Penguin Books, Harmondsworth, 1980).
12. A. C. Browne, 'The Mixed Economy of Day Care: Consumer versus Professional Assessments', *Journal of Social Policy*, vol. 13, pt 3 (1984), pp. 321–39).
13. H. Laming, *Lessons from America: The Balance of Services in Social Care* (Policy Studies Institute, London, 1985), p. 18.
14. R. M. Titmuss, *Commitment to Welfare* (Allen and Unwin, London, 1968), ch. 12.
15. Friedman and Friedman, pp. 263–4.
16. See Titmuss; D. S. Lees, *Health Through Choice* (Institute of Economic Affairs, London, 1961); D. S. Lees, 'Health Through Choice', in *Freedom or Free for All?* (Institute of Economic Affairs, London, 1965).
17. Friedman and Friedman, p. 21.
18. See J. Le Grand, *The Strategy of Equality* (Allen and Unwin, London, 1982).
19. Maynard, 1982, p. 496.
20. A. Walker, 'The Political Economy of Privatisation', in *Privatisation and the Welfare State*, ed. J. Le Grand and R. Robinson (Allen and Unwin, London, 1984), p. 36.
21. R. M. Titmuss, *Essays on the Welfare State* (Allen and Unwin, London, 1963), ch. 1.
22. M. Wilkinson, 'Tax Expenditures and Public Policy in the UK', *Journal of Social Policy*, vol. 15, pt 1 (1986), pp. 23–49.
23. Department of Health and Social Security. *The Reform of Social Security* (HMSO, London, 1985).
24. See J. Higgins, *States of Welfare* (Blackwell, Oxford, 1981), p. 138.
25. K. Weddell, Privatising Social Services in the USA', *Social Policy and Administration*, vol. 20, no. 9 (1986), p. 17.
26. Higgins, p. 140.
27. W. J. McNerney, 'The Control of Health Care Costs in the United States in the Context of Health Insurance Policies', in McLachlan and Maynard, pp. 339–40.
28. Public Information and Cultural Affairs Bureau, *Facts about Japan* (Ministry of Foreign Affairs, Tokyo, 1980, pp. 1–2.
29. See E. G. Dearman, 'Sun City: Care for the Elderly in Arizona', *Social Policy and Administration*, vol. 16, no. 3 (1982), pp. 230–40.
30. N. Gilbert, 'Welfare for Profit: Moral, Empirical and Theoretical Perspectives', *Journal of Social Policy*, vol. 13, pt 1 (1984), p. 64.
31. Laming, p. 18.
32. *Ibid.*, p. 19.

33. Phillips and Vincent, pp. 189–90.
34. M. Dineen, 'Sheltered Homes: A Boom', *Observer*, 13 October 1985.
35. T. Roberts, 'For Those Who Want to Go Out in Style', *Guardian*, 14 December 1985.
36. US Bureau of the Census, *Statistical Abstract of the United States, 1985* (US Bureau of the Census, Washington DC, 1986). Note that these percentages involve some double counting.
37. *The Boston Sunday Globe*, 30 June 1985.
38. *Ibid.*
39. Statistics taken from B. Griffith, G. Rayner and J. Mohan, *Commercial Medicine in London* (Greater London Council, London, 1985), p. 25.
40. See S. Birch, 'Increased Patient Charges in the National Health Service: A Method of Privatizing Primary Care', *Journal of Social Policy*, vol. 15, pt 2 (1986), pp. 163–84).
41. For a fuller treatment, see J. Feder, J. Holahan, R. R. Bovbjerg and J. Hadley, 'Health', in *The Reagan Experiment*, ed. J. L. Palmer and I. V. Sawhill (The Urban Institute Press, Washington DC, 1982).
42. Central Statistical Office, *Social Trends 15* (HMSO, London, 1985), p. 132.
43. T. Roberts, 'For Sale: Run-down Estate, in Need of Some Modernisation, Few Mod Cons. No Reasonable Offer Refused', *The Guardian*, 7 June 1986.
44. R. Robinson, 'Restructuring the Welfare State: An Analysis of Public Expenditure, 1979–80—1984–85, *Journal of Social Policy*, vol. 15, pt 1 (1986) pp. 1–21.
45. *Ibid.*
46. J. Kohl, 'Trends and Problems in Postwar Public Expenditure Development in Western Europe and North America', in *The Development of Welfare States in Europe and America*, eds P. Flora and A. J. Heidenheimer (Transaction Books, New Brunswick, 1981), pp. 313–4.
47. M. Bendick, Jr, 'Vouchers versus Income versus Services: An American Experiment in Housing Policy', *Journal of Social Policy*, vol. 11, pt 3 (1982), pp. 365–78.
48. For a good discussion of various forms of education vouchers, see M. Blaug, 'Education Vouchers: It All Depends What You Mean', in Le Grand and Robinson, pp. 160–76.
49. Walker, p. 36.
50. Le Grand and Robinson, pp. 3–6.
51. R. Klein, 'Private Practice and Public Policy: Regulating the Frontiers', in McLachlan and Maynard, p. 124.
52. N. Gilbert, 'Welfare for Profit: Moral, Empirical and Theoretical Perspectives', *Journal of Social Policy*, vol. 13, pt 1 (1984), p. 64.
53. Judge and Knapp, p. 132.
54. Gilbert, p. 71.
55. *Ibid.*, pp. 71–2.

56. Klein, p. 125.
57. *Ibid.*

CHAPTER 7
1. D. Easton, *The Political System* (Knopf, New York, 1953).
2. C. Wright Mills, *The Power Elite* (Oxford University Press, Oxford, 1956).
3. P. Bachrach and M. S. Baratz, 'The Two Faces of Power', *American Political Science Review*, vol. 56, no. 4 (1962), pp. 942–52.
4. S. Lukes, *Power: A Radical View* (Macmillan, London, 1974).
5. A. Cawson, *Corporatism and Welfare: Social Policy and State Intervention in Britain* (Heinemann, London, 1982), p. 38.
6. *Ibid.*, pp. 38–9.
7. R. Mishra, *The Welfare State in Crisis* (Wheatsheaf, Brighton, 1984), pp. 109–15.
8. R. Miliband, *The State in Capitalist Society*, (Weidenfeld and Nicolson, London, 1969), p. 265.
9. C. Offe, *Contradictions of the Welfare State*, ed. J. Keane Hutchinson, London, 1984), p. 120.
10. R. Nozick, *Anarchy, State and Utopia* (Blackwell, Oxford, 1984); (First edition: Basic Books, New York, 1974).
11. *Ibid.*, p. ix.
12. I. Kristol, *Two Cheers for Capitalism* (Basic Books, New York, 1978), p. 247.
13. I, Kristol, *Reflections of a Neoconservative* (Basic Books, New York, 1983), p. 77.
14. *Ibid.*, p. 76.
15. A. Weale, *Political Theory and Social Policy* (Macmillan, London, 1983), p. 57.
16. *Ibid.*, p. 42.
17. *Ibid.*, pp. 77–8.
18. J. Rawls, *A Theory of Justice* (Clarendon Press, Oxford, 1972), p. 14.
19. A. Walker, *Social Planning: A Strategy for Socialist Welfare* (Blackwell, Oxford, 1984).
20. F. J. Gladstone, *Voluntary Action in a Changing World* (Bedford Square Press, London, 1979).
21. A. Webb and G. Wistow, *Whither State Welfare? Policy and Implementation in the Personal Social Services* (Royal Institute of Public Administration, London, 1982), p. 69.
22. A. Webb, *Collective Action and Welfare Pluralism* (Association of Researchers in Voluntary Action and Community Involvement, London, 1981), p. 9.
23. M. O'Higgins, 'Welfare, Redistribution, and Inequality—Disillusion, Illusion, and Reality' in *In Defence of Welfare*, ed. P. Bean, J. Ferris and D. Whynes (Tavistock, London, 1985), p. 174.
24. *Ibid.*, p. 178.
25. Webb, pp. 13–14.

26.   R. M. Titmuss, *The Gift Relationship: From Human Blood to Social Policy* (Allen and Unwin, London, 1970), p. 212.
27.   *Ibid.*, p. 225.
28.   K. E. Boulding, 'The Boundaries of Social Policy', *Social Work*, vol. 12, no. 1 (1967), p. 7.
29.   See D. Traschys, 'Curbing Public Expenditure: Current Trends', *Journal of Public Policy*, vol. 5, no. 1 (1985), pp. 23–65.
30.   D. E. Ashford, 'Governmental Responses to Budget Scarcity: France', *Policy Studies Journal*, vol. 13, no. 3 (1985), p. 578.
31.   In 1986, Norway's centre-right coalition government was replaced by a minority Labour government.
32.   P. Walters, ' "Distributing Decline": Swedish Social Democrats and the Crisis of the Welfare State', *Government and Opposition*, vol. 20, no. 3 (1985), p. 358.
33.   H. M. Treasury, *The Government's Expenditure Plans, 1985–86 to 1987–88*, Cmnd. 9428, (HMSO, London, 1985).
34.   C. Hartman (ed.), *America's Housing Crisis, What Is to Be Done?* (Routledge and Kegan Paul, Boston, 1983), p. 1.
35.   K. Goudswaard and P. de Jong, 'The Distributional Impact of Current Income Transfer Policies in the Netherlands', *Journal of Social Policy*, vol. 14, pt 3 (1985), p. 371.
36.   *Ibid.*, p. 372.
37.   J. R. Storey, 'Income Security', in *The Reagan Experiment*, ed. J. L. Palmer and I. V. Sawhill (The Urban Institute, Washington DC, 1982), p. 373.
38.   For detailed statistics, see D. L. Bawden and J. L. Palmer, 'Social Policy: Challenging the Welfare State', in *The Reagan Record*, ed. J. L. Palmer and I. V. Sawhill (Ballinger, Cambridge, Mass., 1984); also J. A. Meyer, 'Budget Cuts in the Reagan Administration: A Question of Fairness', in *The Social Contract Revisited*, ed. D. L. Bawden (Urban Institute Press, Washington D.C., 1984).
39.   *Ibid.*, p. 177.
40.   J. L. Palmer and I. V. Sawhill, 'Overview', in Palmer and Sawhill, 1984, p. 13.
41.   See Bawden and Palmer.
42.   L. N. Johansen and J. E. Kolberg, 'Welfare State Regression in Scandinavia? The Development of the Scandinavian Welfare States from 1970 to 1980', in *The Welfare State and Its Aftermath*, ed. S. N. Eisenstadt and O. Ahimeir (Croom Helm, London, 1985), p. 169.
43.   *The Boston Globe*, 20 May 1985, p. 14.
44.   G. E. Peterson, 'The State and Local Sector', in Palmer and Sawhill, 1982, p. 159.
45.   European Centre for Social Welfare Training and Research, *Report of European Expert Meeting on Established Social Services Versus New Social Initiatives*, Vienna, 1985, p. 12 (paper by Emma Fasolo).
46.   *Ibid.*
47.   J. Le Grand, 'Comment on Inequality, Redistribution and Recession', *Journal of Social Policy*, vol. 14, pt 3 (1985), pp. 309–12.

48. Central Statistical Office, *Social Trends*, no. 16 (HMSO), London, 1986).
49. Treasury, *The Next Ten Years: Public Expenditure and Taxation into the 1990s*, Cmnd, 9189 (HMSO, London, 1984).
50. R. Robinson, 'Restructuring the Welfare State: An Analysis of Public Expenditure 1979–80—1984–85', *Journal of Social Policy*, vol. 15, pt 1 (1986), pp. 1–21.
51. *Ibid.*
52. Treasury, *The Government's Expenditure Plans 1985–86 to 1986–87*, Cmnd, 9702 (HMSO, London, 1985).
53. House of Commons, Fourth Report from the Committee of the Social Services, *Paying for the Social Services*, H.C. 395, Session 1983–84 (HMSO, London, 1984).
54. Robinson.
55. Department of Health and Social Security, *The Reform of Social Security*, Cmnd. 9691 (HMSO, London, 1985).
56. S. Danziger and E. Smolensky, 'Income Transfer Policies and the Poor: A Cross-National Perspective', *Journal of Social Policy*, vol. 14, pt 3 (1985), p. 257.
57. M. O'Higgins, 'Inequality, Redistribution and Recession: The British Experience, 1976–1982', *Journal of Social Policy*, vol. 14, pt 3 (1985), pp. 279–307.
58. M. Wilkinson, 'Tax Expenditures and Public Policy in the UK', *Journal of Social Policy*, vol. 15, pt 1 (1986) pp. 23–49.
59. *Ibid.*
60. S. Danziger, P. Gottschalk and E. Smolensky, 'The Effects of Unemployment and Policy Changes on America's Poor', *Journal of Social Policy*, vol. 14, pt 3 (1985), p. 330.
61. US Bureau of the Census figures reported in *The Guardian*, 28 August 1985.
62. Danziger and Smolensky, p. 261.

CHAPTER 8
1. H. Glennerster (ed.), *The Future of the Welfare State* (Heinemann, London, 1983).
2. P. Bean, J. Ferris and D. Whynes (ed.), *In Defence of Welfare* (Tavistock, London, 1985).
3. R. Klein and M. O'Higgins (ed.) *The Future of Welfare* (Blackwell, Oxford, 1985).
4. Bean, Ferris and Whynes, p. xiii.
5. *Ibid.*, p. xi.
6. *Ibid.*
7. Klein and O'Higgins, p. 227.
8. G. Peele, *Revival and Reaction: The Right in Contemporary America* (Oxford University Press, Oxford and New York, 1984).
9. *Ibid.*, p. 51.
10. *Ibid.*, p. 17.
11. R. Levitas (ed.), *The Ideology of the New Right* (Polity Press, Cambridge, 1986).

12. R. Scruton, *The Meaning of Conservatism* (Penguin, Harmondsworth, 1980).
13. I. Kristol, *Two Cheers for Capitalism* (Basic Books, New York, 1978), p. 246.
14. R. Hadley and S. Hatch, *Social Welfare and the Failure of the State* (Allen and Unwin, London, 1981), p. 101.
15. F. J. Gladstone, *Voluntary Action in a Changing World* (Bedford Square Press, London, 1979), p. 115.
16. *Ibid.*
17. Hadley and Hatch, p. 93.
18. N. Gilbert, *Capitalism and the Welfare State* (Yale University Press, New Haven, 1983).
19. *Ibid.*, p. 178.
20. P. Beresford and S. Croft, 'Welfare Pluralism: The New Face of Fabianism', *Critical Social Policy*, no. 9 (1984), p. 25.
21. R. Hadley and M. McGrath, *Going Local* (Bedford Square Press, London, 1980).
22. A. Cawson, *Corporatism and Welfare* (Heinemann, London, 1982), p. 41.
23. *Ibid.*
24. R. Mishra, *The Welfare State in Crisis* (Wheatsheaf, Brighton, 1984), p. 102.
25. *Ibid.*, p. 103.
26. R. Münz and H. Wintersberger, *The Austrian Welfare State: Social Policy and Income Maintenance Programmes Between 1970 and 1984* (European Centre for Social Welfare Training and Research, Vienna, 1984), p. 21.
27. H. L. Wilensky, 'Leftism, Catholicism and Democratic Corporatism: The Role of Political Parties in Recent Welfare State Development', in *The Development of Welfare States in Europe and America*, ed. P. Flora and A. J. Heidenheimer (Transaction Books, New Brunswick, 1981), pp. 345–82.
28. M. G. Schmidt, 'The Welfare State and the Economy in Periods of Economic Crisis: A Comparative Study of Twenty-three OECD Nations', *European Journal of Political Research*, vol. 11, no. 1 (1983), pp. 1–26.
29. Mishra, p. 109.
30. J. O'Connor, *Accumulation Crisis* (Blackwell, New York, 1984), pp. 240–9.
31. J. T. Winkler, 'Corporatism', *Archives Europeennes de sociologie*, vol. 17, no. 1 (1976), pp. 100–36.
32. Cawson, pp. 56–7.
33. M. L. Harrison, 'Themes and Objectives', in *Corporatism and the Welfare State*, ed. M. L. Harrison (Gower, Aldershot, 1984), p. 12.
34. *Ibid.*
35. Cawson, p. 53.
36. M. L. Harrison, 'Corporatism, Incorporation and the Welfare State', in M. L. Harrison, p. 27.
37. *Ibid.*, p. 34.

38. D. Held and J. Krieger, 'Theories of the State: Some Competing Claims', in *The State in Capitalist Europe*, ed. S. Bornstein, D. Held and J. Krieger (Allen and Unwin, London, 1984), p. 13.
39. *Ibid.*
40. A. Deacon, *Social Policy and Socialism: The Struggle for Socialist Relations of Welfare* (Pluto Press, London, 1983), p. 37.
41. Glennerster, p. 1.
42. *Ibid.*, p. 222.
43. Deacon, p. 37.
44. I. Gough, *The Political Economy of the Welfare State* (Macmillan, London, 1979), p. 60.
45. *Ibid.*
46. J. Le Grand, *The Strategy of Equality* (Allen and Unwin, London, 1982), pp. 131–2.
47. M. O'Higgins, 'Welfare, Redistribution and Inequality: Disillusion, Illusion and Reality', in Bean, Ferris and Whynes p. 174.
48. *Ibid.*
49. A Sinfield, 'The Necessity for Full Employment', in Glennerster, pp. 61–2.
50. P. Beresford and S. Croft, 'Welfare Pluralism: The New Face of Fabianism', *Critical Social Policy*, no. 9 (1984), p. 35; see P. Alcock and P. Lee, 'The Socialist Republic of South Yorkshire?', *Critical Social Policy*, vol. 1, no. 2 (1981), pp. 72–93; J. David, 'Walsall and Decentralisation', *Critical Social Policy*, no. 7 (1983), pp. 75–9; Islington Labour Party Working Group on Decentralisation, 'Decentralising Social Services in Islington', Discussion Paper (1983); P. Beresford, 'Patch in Perspective: Decentralising and Democratising Social Services', Battersea Community Action (1983).
51. A. Walker, *Social Planning: A Strategy for Socialist Welfare* (Blackwell, Oxford, 1984).
52. *Ibid.*, pp. 224–5.
53. *Ibid.*, p. 219.
54. M. Friedman and R. Friedman, *The Tyranny of the Status Quo* (Penguin, Harmondsworth, 1985), p. 10.
55. Cawson, p. 81.
56. Walker, p. 220.
57. M. McIntosh, 'Feminism and Social Policy', *Critical Social Policy*, vol. 1, no. 1 (1981), p. 32.
58. *Ibid.*, pp. 40–1.

Bibliography

Abel-Smith, B., *Cost Containment in Health Care: A Study of Twelve European Countries* (Bedford Square Press, London, 1984).

Abel-Smith, B. and Maynard, A., *The Financing, Organisation and Cost of Health Care in the European Community*, European Commission Series, no. 36 (EEC, Brussels, 1978).

Abrams, P., 'Community Care: Some Research Problems and Priorities', *Policy and Politics*, no. 6 (1977).

Abrams, P., 'Social Change, Social Networks and Neighbourhood Care', *Social Work Service*, no. 22 (1980).

Abrams P., Abrams, S. and Davison, J., *Patterns of Neighbourhood Care* (Association of Researchers in Voluntary Action and Community Involvement, Occasional Paper no. 1, 1979).

Allan, G., *Family Life* (Blackwell, Oxford, 1985).

Alt, J., *The Politics of Economic Decline* (Cambridge University Press, Cambridge, 1979).

Ashford, D. E., 'Governmental Responses to Budget Scarcity: France', *Policy Studies Journal*, vol. 13, no. 3 (1985).

Bachrach, P. and Baratz, M. S., 'The Two Faces of Power', *American Political Science Review*, vol. 56, no. 4 (1962).

Bacon, R. and Eltis, W., *Britain's Economic Problems: Too Few Producers* (Macmillan, London, 1976).

Bates, E., *Health Systems and Public Scrutiny (Croom Helm, London, 1983)*.

Bawden, D. L. (ed.), *The Social Contract Revisited* (Urban Institute Press, Baltimore, 1984).

Bean, P., Ferris, J. and Whynes, D. (eds.), *In Defence of Welfare* (Tavistock, London, 1985).

Bell, D., *The End of Ideology* (The Free Press, Illinois, 1960).

Bendick, M. Jr, 'Vouchers versus Income versus Services: An

American Experiment in Housing Policy', *Journal of Social Policy*, vol. 11, pt 3 (1982).

Benington, J., 'Strategies for Change at the Local Level: Some Reflections', *in Community Work One*, ed. D. Jones and M. Mayo (Routledge and Kegan Paul, London, 1974).

Beresford, P. and Croft, S., 'Welfare Pluralism: The New Face of Fabianism', *Critical Social Policy*, no. 9 (1984).

Berger, P. L. and Neuhaus, R. J., *To Empower People: The Role of Mediating Structures in Public Policy* (American Enterprise Institute for Public Policy Research, Washington, DC, 1977).

Berthoud, R., *Challenges to Welfare* (Gower, Aldershot, 1985).

Beyme, K. von and Schmidt, M. G. (eds.), *Policy and Politics in the Federal Republic of Germany* (Gower, Aldershot, 1985).

Birch, S., 'Increased Patient Charges in the National Health Service: A Method of Privatising Primary Care', *Journal of Social Policy*, vol. 15, pt 2 (1986).

Bornstein, S., Held, D. and Krieger, J. (eds.), *The State in Capitalist Europe* (Allen and Unwin, London, 1984).

Bosanquet, N., *After the New Right* (Heinemann, London, 1983).

Boulding, K. E., 'The Boundaries of Social Policy', *Social Work*, vol. 12, no. 1 (1967).

Bovbjerg, R. R. and Holahan, J., *Medicaid in the Reagan Era* (Urban Institute Press, Baltimore, 1982).

Bradshaw, J. and Piachaud, D., *Child Support in the European Community* (Bedford Square Press, London, 1980).

Brayshaw, A. J. *Public Policy and Family Life* (Policy Studies Institute, London, 1980).

Brenton, M., 'Changing Relationships in Dutch Social Services', *Journal of Social Policy*, vol. 11, pt 1 (1982).

Brenton, M., *The Voluntary Sector in British Social Services* (Longman, London, 1985).

Brenton, M. and Jones, C., *The Yearbook of Social Policy in Britain, 1984–5* (Routledge and Kegan Paul, London, 1985).

Briggs, A., 'The Welfare State in Historical Perspective', *European Journal of Sociology*, 11 (1961).

Brittan, S., *The Economic Consequences of Democracy* (Temple Smith, London, 1977).

Brittan, S., 'The Economic Contradictions of Democracy', *British Journal of Political Science*, vol. 5, no. 1 (1975).

Brown, M. and Madge, N., *Despite the Welfare State* (Heinemann, London, 1982).

Browne, A. C., 'The Mixed Economy of Day Care: Consumer Versus Professional Assessments', *Journal of Social Policy*, vol. 13, pt 3 (1984).

Bulmer, M., *Neighbours: The Work of Philip Abrams* (Cambridge University Press, Cambridge, 1986).

Burden, J. and Campbell, M., *Capitalism and Public Policy in the UK: A Marxist Approach* (Croom Helm, London, 1985).

Carrier, J. and Kendall, I., 'Social Policy and Social Change', *Journal of Social Policy*, vol. 2, pt 3 (1973).

Castles, F. G., 'How Does Politics Matter? Structure and Agency in the Determination of Public Policy Outcomes', *European Journal of Political Research*, vol. 9, no. 2 (1981).

Castles, F. G., 'Terra Incognita Australis: A Search for New Directions in Public Policy Analysis', *Government and Opposition*, vol. 20, no. 3 (1985).

Castles, F. G., *The Working Class and Welfare* (Allen and Unwin, Sydney, 1985).

Castles, F. G. (ed.) *The Impact of Parties* (Sage, London, 1982).

Castles, F. G. and McKinlay, R. D., 'Public Welfare Provision: Scandinavia and the Sheer Futility of the Sociological Approach to Politics', *British Journal of Political Science*, vol. 9, no. 2 (1979).

Cawson, A., *Corporatism and Welfare: Social Policy and State Intervention in Britain* (Heinemann, London, 1982).

Charlesworth, A., Wilkin, D. and Durie, A., *Carers and Services: A Comparison of Men and Women Caring for Dependent Elderly People* (Equal Opportunities Commission, Manchester, 1984).

Clark. G. L. and Dear, M., *State Apparatus* (Allen and Unwin, London, 1984).

Commission of the European Communities, *Annual Reports on Social Developments*.

Connolly, W. (ed.) *Legitimacy and the State* (Blackwell, Oxford, 1984).

Conservative Political Centre, *The Future of Marriage* (Conservative Political Centre, London, 1981).

Coughlin, R., *Ideology, Public Opinion and Welfare Policy* (University of California Press, Berkeley, 1980).

Craven, E., Rimmer, L. and Wicks, M., *Family Issues and Public Policy* (Study Commission on the Family, London, 1982).

Dahrendorf, R., 'Effectiveness and Legitimacy', *Political Quarterly*, vol. 51 no. 4 (1980).

Danziger, S., Gottschalk, P. and Smolensky, E., 'The Effects of Unemployment and Policy Changes on America's Poor', *Journal of Social Policy*, vol. 14, pt 3 (1985).

Danziger, S. and Smolensky, E., 'Income Transfer Policies and the Poor: a Cross-National Perspective', *Journal of Social Policy*, vol. 14 pt 3 (1985).

Davidoff, P. and Gould, J., 'Suburban Action: Advocate Planning for an Open Society', *Journal of the American Institute of Planners* (1970).

Deacon, B., *Social Policy and Socialism: The Struggle for Socialist Relations of Welfare* (Pluto Press, London, 1983).

Dearman, E. G., 'Sun City: Care for the Elderly in Arizona', *Social Policy and Administration*, vol. 16, no. 3 (1982).

De Jasay, A., *The State* (Blackwell, Oxford, 1985).

Department of Health and Social Security, *Care in the Community* (HMSO, London, 1981).

Department of Health and Social Security, *Inequalities in Health* (HMSO, London, 1980).

Department of Health and Social Security, *The Reform of Social Security*, Cmnd. 9691 (HMSO, London, 1985).

Dickens, P., Duncan, S., Goodwin, M. and Gray, F., *Housing, States and Localities* (Methuen, New York, 1985).

Dickinson, J. and Russell, R., *Family, Economy and State* (Croom Helm, London, 1985).

Division of Social Affairs of the United Nations Office at Geneva, *Informal Action for the Welfare of the Aged* (United Nations, New York, 1980).

Donnison, D. V., Chapman, V., Meacher, M., Sears, A. and Unwin, K. *Social Policy and Administration* (Allen and Unwin, London, 1965).

Douglas, J., 'The Overloaded Crown', *British Journal of Political Science*, vol. 6, no. 4 (1976).

Douglas, J., *Why Charity? The Case for a Third Sector* (Sage, Beverly Hills, 1983).

Duke, V. and Edgell, S., 'Gender and Social Policy: Impact of the Cuts', *Journal of Social Policy*, vol. 12, pt 3 (1983).

Easton, B., *Social Policy and the Welfare State in New Zealand* (Allen and Unwin, Sydney, 1980).

Eisenstadt, S. N. and Ahimeir, O. (eds.), *The Welfare State and its Aftermath* (Croom Helm, London, 1985).

Equal Opportunities Commission, *Caring for the Elderly and Handicapped: Community Care Policies and Women's Lives* (Equal Opportunities Commission, Manchester, 1982).

Equal Opportunities Commission, *The Experience of Caring for Elderly and Handicapped Dependents: Survey Report* (Equal Opportunities Commission, Manchester, 1980).

Equal Opportunities Commission, *Who Cares for the Carers?* (Equal Opportunities Commission, Manchester, 1982).

Ermisch, J., *The Political Economy of Demography* (Heinemann, London, 1983).

Eversley, D. E. C., 'Some new Aspects òf Ageing in Britain', in *Ageing and the Life Cycle Course in a Cross-Cultural Interdisciplinary Perspective*, ed. T. K. Hareven (Guildford Press, New York, 1982).

Filer, J. H., *Giving in America: Toward a Stronger Voluntary Sector*, Report of the Commission on Private Philanthropy and Public Needs (Washington, DC., 1975).

Finch, J., 'The Deceit of Self-Help: Preschool Playgroups and Working Class Mothers', *Journal of Social Policy*, vol. 13, pt 1 (1984).

Finch, J. and Groves, D., *A Labour of Love* (Routledge and Kegan Paul, London, 1983).

Finch, J. and Groves, D., 'Community Care and the Family: A Case for Equal Opportunities?' *Journal of Social Policy*, vol. 9, pt 4 (1980).

Flora, P. and Heidenheimer, A. J. (eds.), *The Development of Welfare States in Europe and America* (Transaction Books, New Brunswick, 1981).

Forder, A. Caslin, T., Ponton, G. and Walklate, S. *Theories of Welfare* (Routledge and Kegan Paul, London, 1984).

Forsberg, M., *The Evolution of Social Welfare Policy in Sweden* (The Swedish Institute, Stockholm, 1984).

Frankenberg, R., *Communities in Britain* (Penguin Books, Harmondsworth, 1966).

Fraser, D., *The Evolution of the British Welfare State* (Macmillan, London, 1973).

Friedman, M., *Capitalism and Freedom* (University of Chicago Press, Chicago, 1962).

Friedman, M. and Friedman, R., *Free to Choose* (Penguin Books, Harmondsworth, 1980).

Friedman, M. and Friedman, R., *The Tyranny of the Status Quo* (Penguin Books, Harmondsworth, 1985).

Froland, C., Pancoast, D. L., Chapman, N. J. and Kimboko, P. J., *Helping Networks and Human Services* (Sage, Beverly Hills and London, 1981).

Fry, J. (ed.), *Limits of the Welfare State: Critical Views on Post-War Sweden* (Saxon House, Farnborough, 1979).

Furniss, N. and Tilton, T., *The Case for the Welfare State: From Social Security to Social Equality* (Indiana University Press, Bloomington, 1977).

Gartner, A., Greer, C. and Riessman, F. (eds.), *Beyond Reagan: Alternatives for the '80s* (Harper and Row, New York, 1984).

George, V. and Wilding, P., *Ideology and Social Welfare* (Routledge and Kegan Paul, London, 1976).

George, V. and Wilding, P., *The Impact of Social Policy* (Routledge and Kegan Paul, London, 1984).

Gilbert, N., *Capitalism and the Welfare State* (Yale University Press, New Haven, 1983).

Gilbert, N., 'Welfare for Profit: Moral, Empirical and Theoretical Perspectives', *Journal of Social Policy*, vol. 13, pt 1 (1984).

Gilder, G., *Wealth and Poverty* (Bantam Books, New York, 1982).

Ginsburg, N., *Class, Capital and Social Policy* (Macmillan, London, 1979).

Gittins, D., *The Family in Question* (Macmillan, London, 1985).

Gladstone, F. J., *Voluntary Action in a changing World* (Bedford Square Press, London, 1979).

Glazer, N., 'Reagan's Social Policy: A Review', *The Public Interest*, no. 75 (1984).

Glennerster, H. (ed.), *The Future of the Welfare State* (Heinemann, London, 1983).

Glennerster, H., *Paying for Welfare* (Blackwell, Oxford, 1985).

Goodin, R. E., 'Self Reliance versus the Welfare State', *Journal of Social Policy*, vol. 14, pt 1 (1985).

Golding, P. and Middleton, S., *Images of Welfare* (Blackwell, Oxford, 1982).

Goudswaard, K. and de Jong, P., 'The Distributional Impact of Current Income Transfer Policies in the Netherlands', *Journal of Social Policy*, vol. 14, pt 3 (1985).

Gough, I., *The Political Economy of the Welfare State* (Macmillan, London, 1979).

Graham, H., *Women, Health and the Family* (Wheatsheaf, Brighton, 1986).

Grant, W., (ed.), *The Political Economy of Corporatism* (Macmillan, London, 1985).

Graycar, A., *Welfare Politics in Australia* (Macmillan, Melbourne, 1979).

Griffith, B., Rayner, G. and Mohan, J., *Commercial Medicine in London* (Greater London Council, London, 1985).

Habermas, J., *Legitimation Crisis*, trans. T. McCarthy (Heinemann, London, 1976).

Hadley, R. and Hatch, S., *Social Welfare and the Failure of the State* (Allen and Unwin, London, 1981).

Hadley, R. and McGrath, M., *Going Local: Neighbourhood Social Services* (Bedford Square Press, London, 1980).

Hall, S., 'The Great Moving Right Show', *Marxism Today*, January 1979.

Hall, S. and Jacques, M. (eds.), *The Politics of Thatcherism* (Lawrence and Wishart, London, 1983).

Hallett, G., *Housing and Land Policies in West Germany and Britain* (Macmillan, London, 1977).

Ham, C. and Hill, M., *The Policy Process in the Modern Capitalist State* (Wheatsheaf, Brighton, 1984).

Hansen, T. and Newton, K., 'Voluntary Organisations and Community Politics: Norwegian and British Comparisons', *Scandinavian Political Studies*, vol. 8, no. 12 (1985).

Harlow, M., *Private Rented Housing in the United States and Europe* (Croom Helm, London, 1985).

Harris, R. and Seldon, A., *Over-ruled on Welfare* (Institute of Economic Affairs, London, 1979).

Harrison, M. L. (ed.), *Corporatism and the Welfare State* (Gower, Aldershot, 1984).

Hartman, C. (ed.), *America's Housing Crisis: What Is to Be Done?* (Routledge and Kegan Paul, Boston, 1983).

Hatch, S. (ed.), *Decentralisation and Care in the Community* (Policy Studies Institute, London, 1985).

Hatch, S., *Outside the State* (Croom Helm, London, 1980).

Hatch, S. and Mocroft, I., *Components of Welfare* (Bedford Square Press, London, 1983).

Hawkins, K., *Unemployment* (Penguin, Harmondsworth, 1984).

Hayek, F. A., *The Road to Serfdom* (Routledge and Kegan Paul, London, 1944).

Heclo, H., *Modern Social Politics in Britain and Sweden* (Yale University Press, New Haven, 1974).

Heclo, H. and Wildavsky, A., *The Private Government of Public Money* (Macmillan, London, 1981).

Heidenheimer, A. J., Heclo, H. and Adams, C. T., *Comparative Public Policy: The Politics of Social Choice in Europe and America* (St Martin's Press, New York, 1983).

Henwood, M. and Wicks, M., *The Forgotten Army: Family Care and Elderly People* (Family Policy Studies Centre, London, 1984).

Higgins, J., *The Poverty Business: Britain and America* (Blackwell, Oxford, 1978).

Higgins, J., *States of Welfare* (Blackwell and Robertson, Oxford, 1981).

Hughes, N. S. and Lovell, A., 'Breaking the Circuit of Social Control: Lessons in Public Psychiatry from Italy and Franco Basaglia', *Social Science and Medicine*, vol. 23, no. 2 (1986).

Johnson, N., *Voluntary Social Services* (Blackwell, Oxford, 1981).

Jones, C., *Patterns of Social Policy* (Tavistock, London, 1985).

Jones, C., 'Types of Welfare Capitalism', *Government and Opposition*, vol. 20, no. 3 (1985).

Jones, P., *The Thatcher Experiment* (Routledge and Kegan Paul, London, 1980).

Judge, K., 'The Growth and Decline of Social Expenditure', in *Public Expenditure and Social Policy*, ed. A. Walker (Heinemann, London, 1982).

Kaldor, N., *The Economic Consequences of Mrs Thatcher* (Fabian Society, London, 1983).

Kamerman, S. B. and Kahn. A. J. (eds.), *Family Policy: Government and Families in Fourteen Countries* (Columbia University Press, New York, 1978).

King, A., 'Ideas, Institutions and the Policies of Governments', *British Journal of Political Science*, vol. 3, no. 3 (1973).

King, A., 'Overload: Problems of Governing in the 1970s', *Political Studies*, vol. 23, nos. 2 and 3 (1975).

Klein, R. and O'Higgins, M. (eds.), *The Future of Welfare* (Blackwell Oxford, 1985).

Kramer, R. M., *Voluntary Agencies in the Welfare State* (University of California Press, Berkeley, 1981).

Kristol, I., *Reflections of a Neo-conservative* (Basic Books, New York, 1983).

Kristol, I., *Two Cheers for Capitalism* (Basic Books, New York, 1978).

Ladd, E.C., Jnr, and Lipset, S. M., 'Public Opinion and Public Policy', in *The United States in the 1980s*, ed. P. Duignan and A. Rabushka (Hoover Institution, Stanford, 1980).

Lagergren, M., Lundh, H., Orkan, M. and Sanne, C., *Care and Welfare at the Crossroads* (Secretariat for Future Studies, Stockholm, 1982).

Laming, H., *Lessons from America: The Balance of Services in Social Care* (Policy Studies Institute, London, 1985).

Land, H., 'Who Cares for the Family?', *Journal of Social Policy*, vol. 7, pt 3 (1978).

Lane, J.-E., *State and Market: The Politics of the Public and the Private* (Sage, Beverly Hills, 1985).

Lawrence, R., 'Voluntary Action: A Stalking Horse for the Right?', *Critical Social Policy*, vol. 2, no. 3 (1983).

Lees, D. S., 'Health Through Choice', in *Freedom or Free for All?* (Institute of Economic Affairs, London, 1965).

Le Grand, J., 'Comment on Inequality Redistribution and Recession', *Journal of Social Policy*, vol. 14, pt 3 (1985).

Le Grand, J., *The Strategy of Equality* (Allen and Unwin, London, 1982).

Le Grand, J. and Robinson. R. (eds.), *Privatisation and the Welfare State* (Allen and Unwin, London, 1984).

Leonard, P., 'Restructuring the Welfare State', *Marxism Today*, December 1979.

Levitas, R. (ed.), *The Ideology of the New Right* (Polity Press, Cambridge, 1986).

Linton, M., *The Swedish Road to Socialism* (Fabian Society, London, 1985).

Lister, R. (ed.), *Family Policy: Alternative Viewpoints* (Child Poverty Action Group, London, 1983).

Litwak, E. and Szelenyi, I., 'Primary Group Structures and Their Functions: Kin, Neighbours and Friends', *American Sociological Review*, vol. 34, no. 4 (1969).

London conference of Socialist Economists Group, *The Alternative Economic Strategy* (Conference of Socialist Economists Books, London, 1980).

London Edinburgh Weekend Return Group, *In and Against the State* (Pluto Press, London, 1979).

Loney, M., Boswell, D. and Clarke, J. (eds.), *Social Policy and Social Welfare* (Open University Press, Milton Keynes, 1983).

Lukes, S., *Power: A Radical View* (Macmillan, London, 1974).

McIntosh, M., 'Feminism and Social Policy', *Critical Social Policy* vol. 1, no. 1 (1981).

McLachlan, G. and Maynard, A. (eds.), *The Public/Private Mix for Health: The Relevance and Effects of Change* (Nuffield Provincial Hospitals Trust, London, 1982).

Mangen, S. (ed.), *Mental Health Care in the European Community* (Croom Helm, London, 1985).

Mann, M., *Socialism Can Survive* (Fabian Society, London, 1985).

Manning, N. (ed.), *Social Problems and Welfare Ideology* (Gower, Aldershot, 1985).

Marmor, T. R. and Christianson, J. B., *Health Care Policy* (Sage, Beverly Hills, 1982).

Marshall, T. H., *The Right to Welfare and Other Essays* (Heinemann, London, 1981).

Marshall, T. H., *Social Policy* (Hutchinson, London, 1975).

Marshall, T. H., 'Value Problems of Welfare Capitalism', *Journal of Social Policy*, vol. 1, no. 1 (1972).

Martin, J. and Roberts, C., *Women and Employment: A Lifetime Perspective* (Department of Employment/Office of Population Censuses and Surveys, London, 1984).

Matthiessen, P. C., *Factsheet Denmark: The Demographic Situ-

ation (Royal Danish Ministry of Foreign Affairs, Copenhagen, 1981).

Maynard, A., *Health Care in the European Community* (Croom Helm, London, 1975).

Maynard, A., 'Privatising the National Health Service', *Lloyds Bank Review*, no. 148 (1983).

Miliband, R., *Capitalist Democracy in Britain* (Oxford University Press, Oxford, 1984).

Miliband, R., *The State in Capitalist Society* (Weidenfeld and Nicolson, London, 1969).

Mills, C. W., *The Power Elite* (Oxford University Press, 1956).

Mishra, R., *Society and Social Policy* (Macmillan, London, 1977).

Mishra, R., *The Welfare State in Crisis* (Wheatsheaf Books, Brighton, 1984).

Mommsen, W. J. (ed.), *The Emergence of the Welfare State in Britain and Germany* (Croom Helm, London, 1981).

Morgan, P. A., 'Constructing Images of Deviance', in *Marital Violence*, ed. N. Johnson (Routledge and Kegan Paul, London, 1985).

Moroney, R. M., *The Family and the State* (Longman, London, 1976).

Morris, R., 'The Future challenge to the Past: The Case of the American Welfare State', *Journal of Social Policy*, vol. 13, pt 4 (1984).

Mount, F., *The Subversive Family: An Alternative History of Love and Marriage* (Jonathan Cape, London, 1982).

Munday, B., *European Expert Meeting on Established Social Services Versus New Social Initiatives* (European Centre for Social Welfare Training and Research, Vienna, 1985).

Münz, R. and Wintersberger, H., *The Austrian Welfare State: Social Policy and Income Maintenance Programmes Between 1970 and 1984* (European Centre for Social Welfare Training and Research, Vienna, 1984).

Murray, C., *Losing Ground* (Basic Books, New York, 1984).

Myrdal, G., *Beyond the Welfare State* (Methuen, London, 1960).

Myrdal, G., 'The Place of Values in Social Policy', *Journal of Social Policy*, vol. 1, pt 1 (1972).

National Council for Voluntary Organisations, *Beyond the Welfare State* (Bedford Square Press, London, 1980).

Navarro, V., *Class Struggle, the State and Medicine* (Martin Robertson, London, 1978).

Navarro, V., *Medicine under Capitalism* (Croom Helm, London, 1976).

Nissel, M. and Bonnerjea, L., *Family Care of the Handicapped Elderly: Who Pays?* (Policy Studies Institute, London, 1982).

Norwegian Institute of Gerontology, *Elderly Norwegians* (NIG, Oslo, 1984).

Nowotny, H. (ed.), *Social Concerns for the 1980s* (European Centre for Social Welfare Training and Research, Vienna, 1984).

Nozick, R., *Anarchy, State and Utopia* (Blackwell, Oxford, 1984).

O'Connor, J., *Accumulation Crisis* (Blackwell, New York, 1984).

O'Connor, J., *The Fiscal Crisis of the State* (St Martin's Press, New York, 1973).

Offe, C., *Contradictions of the Welfare State*, ed. J. Keane (Hutchinson, London, 1984).

O'Higgins, M., 'Inequality, Redistribution and Recession: The British Experience, 1976–1982', *Journal of Social Policy*, vol. 14, pt 3 (1985).

Organisation for Economic Co-operation and Development, *Measuring Health Care* (OECD, Paris, 1985).

Organisation for Economic Co-operation and Development, *High Unemployment: A Challenge for Income Support Policies* (OECD, Paris, 1984).

Organisation for Economic Co-operation and Development, *The Welfare State in Crisis* (OECD, Paris, 1981).

Organisation for Economic Co-operation and Development, *Social Expenditure 1960–1990* (OECD, Paris, 1985).

Page, R., *Stigma* (Routledge and Kegan Paul, London, 1984).

Palmer, J. L. and Sawhill, I. V. (eds.), *The Reagan Experiment* (The Urban Institute, Washington, DC, 1982).

Palmer, J. L. and Sawhill, I. V. (eds.), *The Reagan Record* (Ballinger, Cambridge, Mass., 1984).

Pancoast, D. L., Parker, P. and Froland, C. (eds.), *Rediscovering Self-Help: Its Role in Social Care* (Sage, Beverly Hills, 1983).

Parker, G., *With Due Care and Attention* (Family Policy Studies Centre, London, 1985).

Paukert, L., *The Employment and Unemployment of Women in OECD Countries* (OECD, Paris, 1984).

Paul, J. (ed.), *Reading Nozick* (Blackwell, Oxford, 1982).

Peele, G., *Revival and Reaction: The Right in Contemporary America* (Oxford University Press, Oxford and New York, 1984).

Phillips, D. R., Vincent, J. A., assisted by Blacksell, S., 'Petit Bourgeois Care: Private Residential Care for the Elderly', *Policy and Politics*, vol. 14, no. 2 (1986).

Pinker, R., *The Idea of Welfare* (Heinemann, London, 1979).

Pinker, R., 'Populism and the Social Services', *Social Policy and Administration*, vol. 18, no. 1 (1984).

Pinker, R., *Social Theory and Social Policy* (Heinemann, London, 1971).

Piven, F. F. and Cloward, R., *The New Class War: Reagan's Attack on the Welfare State and its Consequences* (Pantheon, New York, 1982).

Piven, F. and Cloward, R., *Regulating the Poor* (Tavistock, London, 1972).

Purkis, A., *Voluntary Organisations and Government: Reflections from Reagan's America* (National Council for Voluntary Organisations, London, 1985).

Rawls, J., *A Theory of Justice* (Clarendon Press, Oxford, 1972).

Richardson, A., *Participation* (Routledge and Kegan Paul, London, 1983).

Richardson, A., *Working with Self-Help Groups* (Bedford Square Press, London, 1984).

Rimlinger, G. V., *Welfare Policy and Industrialization in Europe, America and Russia* (John Wiley, New York, 1971).

Rimmer, L. and Popay, J., *Employment Trends and the Family* (Study Commission on the Family, London, 1982).

Robinson, D. and Henry, S., *Self-Help and Health* (Martin Robertson, Oxford, 1977).

Robinson, R., 'Restructuring the Welfare State: An Analysis of Public Expenditure', *Journal of Social Policy*, vol. 15, pt 1 (1986).

Room, G., *The Sociology of Welfare* (Blackwell, Oxford, 1979).

Rose, H., 'Rereading Titmuss: The Sexual Division of Welfare', *Journal of Social Policy*, vol. 10, pt 4 (1981).

Rose, H. and Rose, S., 'Moving Right Out of Welfare and the Way Back', *Critical Social Policy*, vol. 2, no. 1 (1982).

Rose, R., *Understanding Big Government* (Sage, London, 1984).

Rose, R. (ed.), *Challenge to Governance: Studies in Overloaded Politics* (Sage, London, 1980).

Rose, R. and Peters, G., *Can Governments Go Bankrupt?* (Macmillan, London, 1979).

Rossiter, C. and Wicks, M., *Crisis or Challenge, Family Care, Elderly People and Social Policy* (Study Commission on the Family, London, 1982).

Saville, J., 'The Welfare State: An Historical Approach', *New Researcher*, vol. 3 (1957).

Schmidt, M. G., 'The Welfare State and the Economy in Periods of Economic Crisis: A Comparative Study of Twenty-three

OECD Nations', *European Journal of Political Research*, vol. 11, no. 1 (1983).

Scruton, R., *The Meaning of Conservatism* (Penguin Books, Harmondsworth, 1980).

Shanas, E., Townsend, P., Wedderburn, D., Milhøj, P. Stehouwer, J. and Friis, H., *Old People in Three Industrial Societies* (Routledge and Kegan Paul, London, 1968).

Shonfield, A., *In Defence of the Mixed Economy*, ed. Z. Shonfield (Oxford University Press, 1984).

Skocpol, T., *States and Social Revolutions* (Cambridge University Press, London, 1979).

Steinfels, P., *The Neo-Conservatives: The Men Who are Changing American Politics* (Simon and Schuster, New York, 1979).

Storey, J. R., *Older Americans in the Reagan Era* (Urban Institute Press, Baltimore, 1983).

Swedish Institute, *Child Care Programmes in Sweden* (The Swedish Institute, Stockholm, 1984).

Swedish Institute, *Old-Age Care in Sweden* (The Swedish Institute, Stockholm, 1984).

Taylor-Gooby, P., *Public Opinion, Ideology and State Welfare* (Routledge and Kegan Paul, London, 1985).

Thane, P., *The Foundations of the Welfare State* (Longman, London, 1982).

Thompson, C., *Sharing Caring: Caring, Equal Opportunities and the Voluntary Sector* (National Council for Voluntary Organisations, London, 1985).

Titmuss, R. M. *Commitment to Welfare* (Allen and Unwin, London, 1968).

Titmuss, R. M. *Essays on the Welfare State* (Allen and Unwin, London, 1963).

Titmuss, R. M. *The Gift Relationship: From Human Blood to Social Policy* (Allen and Unwin, London, 1970).

Titmuss, R. M. *Income Distribution and Social Change* (Allen and Unwin, London, 1962).

Titmuss, R. M. *Social Policy: An Introduction* (Allen and Unwin, London, 1974).

Townsend, P. and Davidson, N., *Inequalities in Health* (Penguin, Harmondsworth, 1982).

Traschys, D., 'Curbing Public Expenditure: Current Trends', *Journal of Public Policy*, vol. 5, no. 1 (1985).

Twelvetrees, A., 'Lessons from America: Alinsky's Legacy', *Community Care*, 22 May 1986.

Twelvetrees, A., 'Lessons from America: Corporation Clues', *Community Care*, 15 May 1986.

Treasury, *The Next Ten Years: Public Expenditure and Taxation Into the 1990s*, Cmnd. 9189 (HMSO, London, 1984).

Treasury, *The Government's Expenditure Plans, 1985–6 to 1987–88*, Cmnd, 9428 (HMSO, London, 1985).

Voluntary Organisations Personal Social Service Group, *The Future of the Social Services* (VOPSSG, London, 1986).

Walker, A. (ed.), *Community Care* (Blackwell, Oxford, 1982).

Walker, A., *Social Planning: A Strategy for Socialist Welfare* (Blackwell, Oxford, 1984).

Walker, R., Lawson, R. and Townsend, P., *Responses to Poverty: Lessons from Europe* (Gower, Aldershot, 1984).

Walters, P., ' "Distributing Decline": Swedish Social Democrats and the Crisis of the Welfare State', *Government and Opposition*, vol. 20, no. 3 (1985).

Walters, P., 'Sweden's Public Sector Crisis, Before and After the 1982 Election', *Government and Opposition*, vol. 18, no. 1 (1983).

Weale, A., *Political Theory and Social Policy* (Macmillan, London, 1983).

Webb, A., *Collective Action and Welfare Pluralism* (Association of Researchers in Voluntary Action and Community Involvement, London, 1981).

Webb, A. and Wistow, G., *Whither State Welfare? Policy and Implementation in the Personal Social Services* (Royal Institute of Public Administration, London, 1982).

· Weddell, K., 'Privatising Social Services in the USA', *Social Policy and Administration*, vol. 20, no. 1 (1986).

West, P., 'The Family, the Welfare State and Community Care: Political Rhetoric and Public Attitudes', *Journal of Social Policy*, vol. 13, pt 4 (1984).

Wilensky, H. L., *The Welfare State and Equality* (University of California Press, Berkeley, 1975).

Wilensky, H. L. and Lebeaux, C. N., *Industrial Society and Social Welfare* (The Free Press, New York, 1965).

Wilkinson, M., 'Tax Expenditures and Public Policy in the UK', *Journal of Social Policy*, vol. 15, pt 1 (1986).

Willmott, P., *Social Networks, Informal Care and Public Policy* (Policy Studies Institute, London, 1986).

Wilson, E., *Women and the Welfare State* (Tavistock, London, 1977).

Wilson, T. and Wilson, D. J., *The Political Economy of the Welfare State* (Allen and Unwin, London, 1982).

Winkler, J. T., 'Corporatism', *Archives Européennes de Sociologie*, vol. 17, no. 1 (1976).

Wolfe, A., *The Limits of Legitimacy* (The Free Press, New York, 1977).
Wolfenden, J., *The Future of Voluntary Organisations* (Croom Helm, London, 1978).

Index of Names

Titmuss, R. M. 11, 12, 13, 17, 30,
  45, 58, 131, 132, 137, 162
Townsend, P. 30, 45, 47
Traschys, D. 218
Twelvetrees, A. 99, 100

Vaughan, G. 120
Veit-Wilson, J. 26
Vincent, J. A. 141

Walker, A. 61, 66, 136–7, 145–6,
  158, 195, 196, 198
Walters, P. 218
Weale, A. 156, 157
Webb, A. 158, 161
Weddell, K. 138–9
Wedderburn, D. 4, 30

Whitehouse, M. 87
Whynes, D. 178
Wilding, P. 32
Wilensky, H. L. 7, 8, 11, 12, 22,
  23, 186
Wilkin, D. 71, 72, 73
Wilkinson, M. 138, 175
Wilmott, P. 89, 90, 208
Wilson, E. 44
Winkler, J. T. 187
Wintersberger, H. 81, 185
Wistow, G. 158
Wolfe, A. 37, 38
Wollert, R. 102, 103

Young, K. 59
Young, M. 208

Index of Subjects

altruism, 162
Australian governments, 165
Austria, corporatism in, 14,
    184–6
autonomy, 156–7

Beveridge Report, 17, 35
Britain, corporatism in, 186;
    economic problems of, 18, 32;
    government overload in, 33–6;
    labour movement in, 9, 24;
    private markets in, 124–49;
    voluntary sector in, 94–123
budget deficits, 39
bureaucracy, 8, 9, 57, 60–1, 180,
    182

captialism, 2, 4, 5, 28, 36–44,
    152–3, 155, 190; accumulation
    in, 6, 37–40, 124, 190;
    accumulation crisis in, 32–3
charges, 143, 169–70
Combined Federal Campaign, 111
commercial sector, 2, 55–63,
    124–49, 159, 160, 162, 183–4
communism, 17–18, 190, 192–3
Community Action Agencies, 97
community care, 62, 65–9, 70, 93
Community Development
    Corporations, 100
Community Development
    Projects, 60, 100–1
Confederation of British Industry,
    32
Conservative Party, 48, 54

continental pattern, 21, 144–5
convergence, 25–9
corporatism, 14, 151–2, 184–9,
    197
cost-sharing, 132, 143, 169

decentralisation, 58–61, 171, 182
Democratic Party, 24, 46
deregulation, 58, 147, 171
differentiated welfare state, 14
diffusion, 10
Dinnington Project, 91
dirigism, 158–9
divorce, 78–9

economic growth, 18, 31, 164
Economic Opportunity Act, 24
economic problems, 31–3
employment, 3; of women, 76–8;
    public, 170–1 (see also
    unemployment)
end of ideology, 27–9
equality, 36, 47, 134–7, 155–7,
    159–60, 174–5, 180–1, 191,
    193–4
Equal Opportunities Commission,
    71–3
European Centre for Social Work
    Training and Research, 56
externalities, 131

Fabians, 27, 30, 31; and defence
    of the welfare state, 45–6,
    190–1; and socialism, 3, 155–6,
    189–96

241

OECD, 31, 39, 163–7, 196
oil crisis, 31
opinion polls, 50–3

participation, 58–61, 96–108, 161–2, 181–2, 195
particulier initiatif, 112–14
planning, 61, 158–9, 195–6
Plowden Report, 30
Policy Studies Institute, 71
political parties, 7, 8, 9
political pluralism, 27, 60, 150–1
pressure groups, 8, 9, 34, 108–11
private markets, 52, 124–49, 197; choice and, 132–4; efficiency and, 127–32; equality and, 134–7; in health services, 142–4; in housing, 144; in residential accommodation, 141–2
privatisation, 88, 137, 139, 146

Reagan administration, 110, 121–2, 146, 166
retrenchment, 54, 62–3, 146, 162–77

Scandinavian pattern, 21, 145–6
Second World War, 3, 4, 15–19
self-help, 56, 101–8, 171
social class, 8, 9, 37, 44, 60, 152–3, 187–9, 190, 193
Social Democratic Party, 48
social expenditure, 21–5, 162–75, 200
socialism, 3, 28, 61, 155–6, 189–200
state, corporatist views of, 151–2; curtailing the role of, 162–7; Marxist views of, 152–3; minimal, 153–5; pluralist views of, 150–1
statutory sector, 2, 52, 5.–63; advantages of, 157–62; commercial sector and, 146–9;

informal sector and, 91–3; voluntary sector and, 117–23
Sweden, and corporatism, 14, 185–6; social democracy in, 22, 165

tax expenditures, 144, 174–5
tax rebellions, 38–9, 48–9
Thatcher government, 46, 48, 122

unemployment, 17, 24, 26, 31, 33, 165, 173, 175, 191, 194–5 (see also employment)
United States, corporatism in, 186–7; occupational welfare in, 138–9; private markets in, 124–49; voluntary sector in, 94–123; as welfare state laggard, 4, 5, 9, 10, 12, 22–5

vendorism, 119
Voluntary Organisations Personal Social Services Group, 123
voluntary sector, 2, 55–63, 94–123; commercial sector and, 116–17; definition of, 94–6; informal sector and, 115–16; statutory sector and, 117–23
vouchers, 126, 135, 145–6

War on Poverty, 24, 30, 60, 97
welfare backlash, 48–54
welfare state, 3–29; and capitalism, 2, 4, 5, 6, 13–14, 19–20, 26, 36–8, 188; in crisis, 1, 30–54, 200; development of, 4–11, 15–25; support for, 1, 45–54, 157–62, 178–9, 191
Wolfenden Report, 55–6, 109, 115–16
workfare, 169
working class pressure, 8, 24–5, 43–4, 190, 193, 198